RECON ACADEMY

FILE NO. 578249

PREP
SQUADRON

BY CHRIS EVERHEART
ILLUSTRATED BY ARCANA STUDIO

ACCESS GRANTED >>>>

Raintree is an imprint of Capstone Global Library Limited, a company
incorporated in England and Wales having its registered office at 264
Banbury Road, Oxford, OX2 7DY – Registered company number: 6695582

www.raintree.co.uk
myorders@raintree.co.uk

Text © Capstone Global Library Limited 2020
The moral rights of the proprietor have been asserted.

Edited by Donnie Lemke
Designed by Brann Garvey and Bob Lentz
Original illustrations © Capstone Global Library Limited 2020
Originated by Capstone Global Library Ltd
Printed and bound in India

ISBN 978 1 4747 8432 0
23 22 21 20 19
10 9 8 7 6 5 4 3 2 1

British Library Cataloguing in Publication Data
A full catalogue record for this book is available from the British Library.

〉CONTENTS

〉〉〉〉
ENTER

ジェイ

JAY /GADGETRY

Born into a world of rising threat —

As they grew up, each member developed a unique ability . . .

— they witnessed terror strike the safety of their town.

FORENSICS

MARTIAL ARTS

COMPUTERS

GADGETRY

In the corridors of Seaside High, the four of them united.

They combined their skills and formed the most high-tech and secret security force on Earth.

RECON ACADEMY

CONTINUE >>>>

FILE NO. 5782H9

SECTION

1

ACCESS GRANTED 〉〉〉〉

JAY
GADGETRY

128718
293829
9283
98289
89
1
109201
192091
1992

It's not that kind of training.

We're supposed to work together to get inside.

You keep breaking the rules.

Look who's talking, Haz!

Why aren't you wearing your fatigues?

You know I have sensitve skin, man.

Those uniforms make me itch for days.

Fine.

Good! Now follow my hand signals.

This means to freeze.

This means get in file formation.

And this means to enter.

SECTION

ACCESS GRANTED ⟩⟩⟩⟩

JAY
GADGETRY

128718
293829
9283
98289
89
1
109201
192091
1992

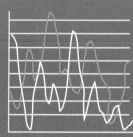

Sounds like you guys have some things to work out.

I'm out of here.

I am serious, Ryker.

We should rethink the entry training.

Why do we have high-tech equipment if we're not going to use it?

If you're not interested in training, Johnson, then just quit the team!

Johnson?

He never uses my last name. What's he so angry about?

22

SECTION

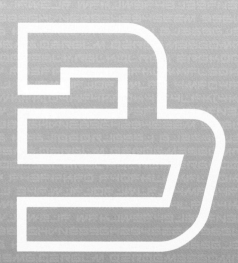

3

ACCESS GRANTED 〉〉〉〉

JAY
GADGETRY

128718
293829
9283
98289
89
1
109201
192091
1992

1827178   198291821   918298

1827178   198291821   918298

Back at Ryker's house . . .

Stop texting me, Jay! We'll talk tomorrow.

TO: JAY

I'M GOING BACK TO SLEEP NOW

Joker.

Doesn't he know the team needs to rest?

At the naval base . . .

ZZZZRT!!

ZZZZRT!

CLINK!

33

34

At the naval base . . .

No security system?

This part will be easier than I thought.

Uh-oh! A high-tech laser net.

I'd better take my time.

That's what I thought until I ordered him not to text anymore.

Then he texted "This drill is too dangerous."

What drill?

I wonder what he's up to . . .

Nice try, Ryker.

But military security is no match for Super-Jay.

SECTION

4

ACCESS GRANTED 〉〉〉〉

JAY
GADGETRY

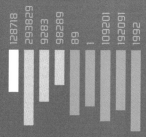

| 8579 |
| 1564574 |
| 109201 |
| 192091 |
| 1992 |
| 745979 |

128718 263829 9283 98286 89 1 109201 192061 1992

Then . . .

Who says gadgets don't come in handy?

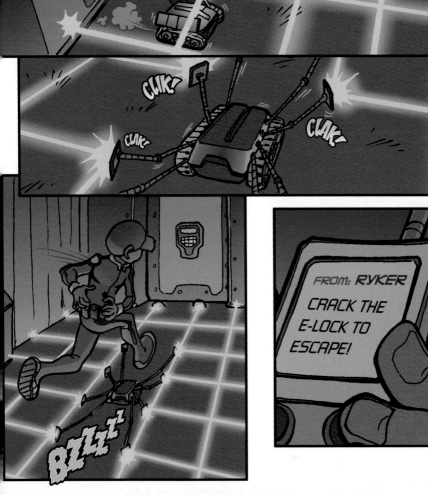

41

His last message said 'Military security'. He must be at the naval base.

Who knows what he's got himself into . . .

I'll never get out of here if I have to crack the code.

Ryker knows I'm terrible at codes!

But I might have another way.

43

Back inside the base . . .

First time in action, mister power pack.

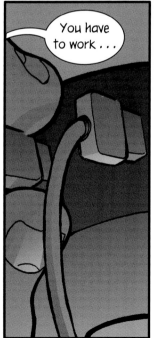

You have to work . . .

. . . or neither of us gets out of here.

A little Jay-tricity, and . . .

ZZZRT!

47

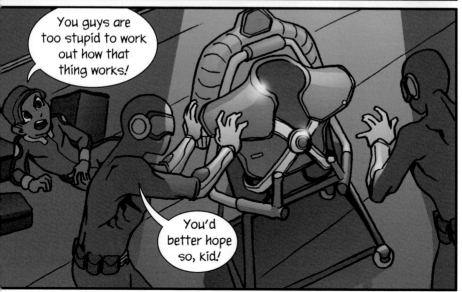

A moment later . . .

Psst!

They're stealing the Weapon-Z. We have to do something!

SPYSPACE
a place for international spies

PROFILE

NAME: Jeremiah Johnson

CODE NAME: Jay

AGE: 13

HEIGHT: 1.65 metres

WEIGHT: 54 kilograms

EYES: brown

HAIR: none

SPY ORG: Recon Academy

SPECIAL ABILITIES: The group's gadget guru and a totally gnarly skateboarder

FAVOURITES: My pack filled with tools and original inventions and, of course, my skateboard

QUOTE: "I consider skateboarding an art form, a lifestyle and a sport." – Tony Hawk

PHOTOS

HOME   SEARCH   BROWSE   LOGOUT

FRIENDS

 Emmi   Haz   Ryker   007

BLOG
recent posts   see all

Hey, guys! Sorry for being such a grump lately. Anyway, I've learned my lesson...

...and knowing is half the battle, right?

Don't worry, Jay. We all get a little crazy sometimes. Remember when Ryker had a crush on the new exchange student? We didn't hear from him for two weeks!

Yeah, remember – Hey! Let's not bring that up again. Besides, we're talking about Jay. He's finally learned that old-fashioned tactics are better than silly gadgets.

Ryker, you might want to look outside...

Jay! What have you done?! My bike just took off down the street by itself!

Oh, that's just a little gadget of mine. But I'm sure you'll be able to catch it the old-fashioned way.

CASE: "Prep Squadron"
CASE NUMBER: 9781474784320
AGENT: Jay
ORGANIZATION: Recon Academy

SUBJECT: Infiltration tactics

OVERVIEW: Members of the Shadow Cell are highly organized and difficult to capture. Their hideouts range from vast underground networks of tunnels to titanium-enforced chambers, secured by high-tech security locks. Knowledge of infiltration tactics is necessary to permeate these locales and secure these dangerous criminals.

INTELLIGENCE:

lockpicking act of unlocking something that is not meant to be opened

hacking process of penetrating electronic or computer security measures

circumvent go around or bypass in order to gain access to something

HISTORY:

Infiltration tactics have existed since the invention of security devices. Wooden locks were used as far back as 4,000 years ago in ancient Egypt.

Lockpicking uses devices that circumvent physical security measures such as padlocks. Keys designed to open locks have a specific pattern of raised edges that hit the pins within the tumbler in the exact combination required to open it. Thus, lockpicks take the place of the key, although they require much more effort. The tumbler (mechanism inside a lock) is picked (opened) by manipulating the pins inside using a lockpick. Then small metal tools called torsion wrenches twist the cylinder, opening the lock.

Hacking is the penetration of electronic security measures. In order to access classified information, a spy must penetrate electronic defences such as firewalls. A firewall is a piece of computer software that uses a set of rules to allow or deny access to information. Firewalls are named after walls in buildings designed to contain fires and prevent damage being done to surrounding areas.

CONCLUSION:

Recon Academy trains its recruits in only the newest, most advanced methods of security system circumvention, whether electronic or physical.

〉 ABOUT THE AUTHOR

Chris Everheart always dreamed of interesting places, fascinating people and exciting adventures. He is still a dreamer. He enjoys writing thrilling stories about young heroes who live in a world that doesn't always understand them. Chris lives in Minnesota, USA, with his family. He plans to travel to every continent on Earth, see interesting places, meet fascinating people and have exciting adventures.

〉 ABOUT THE ILLUSTRATOR

Arcana Studios, Inc. was founded by Sean O'Reilly in British Columbia, Canada, in 2004. Arcana has since established itself as Canada's largest comic book and graphic novel publisher. A nomination for a Harvey Award and winning the "Schuster Award for Top Publisher" are just a couple of Arcana's accolades. The studio is known as a quality publisher for independent comic books and graphic novels.

) GLOSSARY

achieved gained, or did something successfully

assuming believing something to be true

cooperate work together

fatigues uniforms, usually for people in the military

forensic using science to help investigate and solve crimes

hacked gained access to computer information illegally

hinges movable metal joints on a window or door that allow it to open and close

) DISCUSSION QUESTIONS

1. Find some examples in the story where the Recon squad works as a team to get something done. Why is teamwork important?

2. In the beginning of the story, Jay disregards team exercises. But at the end of the story, Jay has realized the importance of teamwork. What do you think caused Jay to change his mind?

3. Hazmat doesn't always wear the same uniform that the other Recon Academy members wear. Do you think school uniforms are a good idea? Why or why not?

) WRITING PROMPTS

1. Jay is tricked into doing Shadow Cell's dirty work for them. Have you ever been tricked? What happened? How was the situation resolved?

2. The Recon team uses lots of high-tech gadgets such as sticky bombs and code-cracking devices. Think of a new gadget for team Recon and write about what it does and how it works. Then draw a picture of your new gadget.

3. What would have happened to Jay if the police had arrived when he was tricked into infiltrating the military base? Imagine you are Jay and write an explanation for your actions, showing how Shadow Cell manipulated you. What evidence would help to prove your innocence?

CHECK OUT MORE

ACTION AND ADVENTURE!

> SHADOW CELL SCAM

> NUCLEAR DISTRACTION

> THE HIDDEN FACE OF FREN-Z